Here's what some of today [barcode] **D0978529**
saying about the *Holy Bibl*

"*The Living Bible* has been used by God around the world for many years to introduce people to the Scriptures. It makes the Bible come alive in a way that is easily understood by even the newest Christian. Now I am pleased to recommend the New Living Translation for even greater readability and accuracy."

BILLY GRAHAM
Billy Graham Evangelistic Association

"Nothing illuminates the way God wants us to live more than the Bible. The New Living Translation is an excellent way to communicate God's truth to people of all ages and spiritual backgrounds."

JOSH McDOWELL
Josh McDowell Ministries

"People are seeking spiritual guidance today more than ever—and there's no better way for them to gain insight than by using God's Word. The New Living Translation communicates the good news of God's promises and will leave a lasting impact on whoever reads it."

GREG LAURIE
Harvest Crusades

"The New Living Translation opens up Scripture so all people can more easily understand the life-changing truth that transforms the nonbeliever into a devoted follower of Christ."

BILL HYBELS
Willow Creek Community Church
South Barrington, Illinois

"My study of Romans moved me to long for more of God's truth illuminating my heart and mind, to repent more deeply, revel in Christ's redemption, and make renewed commitments to lead an ethical life that enhances harmony in the church and builds others in the faith. I enthusiastically recommend the New Living Translation."

ARTHUR EVANS GAY
President, World Relief Corporation
Past President, National Association of Evangelicals

"I'm grateful for a modern translation of the Scriptures like the New Living Translation. This is the word of life, so it has to be given in the language of the people—their heart language—in clear, under-standable, accurate words."

HYATT MOORE
U. S. Director, Wycliffe Bible Translators

LIVING WORDS

Living Words

TYNDALE HOUSE PUBLISHERS, INC.
WHEATON, ILLINOIS

CONTENTS

With 40 million copies in print, *The Living Bible* has been meeting a great need in people's hearts for more than thirty years. But even good things can be improved, so ninety evangelical scholars from various theological backgrounds and denominations were commissioned in 1989 to begin revising *The Living Bible.* The end result of this seven-year process is the *Holy Bible,* New Living Translation—a general-purpose translation that is accurate, easy to read, and excellent for study.

The goal of any Bible translation is to convey the meaning of the ancient Hebrew and Greek texts as accurately as possible to the modern reader. The New Living Translation is based on the most recent scholarship in the theory of translation. The challenge for the translators was to create a text that would make the same impact in the life of modern readers that the original text had for the original readers. In the New

Living Translation, this is accomplished by translating entire thoughts (rather than just words) into natural, everyday English. The end result is a translation that is easy to read and understand and that accurately communicates the meaning of the original text.

We believe that this new translation, which combines the latest in scholarship with the best in translation style, will speak to your heart. We present the New Living Translation with the prayer that God will use it to speak his timeless truth to the church and to the world in a fresh, new way.

The Publishers
January 1996

HOLY BIBLE
NEW LIVING TRANSLATION
BIBLE TRANSLATION TEAM

PENTATEUCH
  Daniel I. Block, *General Reviewer*
  The Southern Baptist Theological Seminary

GENESIS
Allan Ross, *Trinity Episcopal Seminary*
John Sailhamer, *Northwestern College*
Gordon Wenham, *The Cheltenham and Gloucester College of Higher
  Education*

EXODUS
Robert Bergen, *Hannibal-LaGrange College*
Daniel I. Block, *The Southern Baptist Theological Seminary*
Eugene Carpenter, *Bethel College, Mishawaka, Indiana*

LEVITICUS
David Baker, *Ashland Theological Seminary*
Victor Hamilton, *Asbury College*
Kenneth Mathews, *Beeson Divinity School, Samford University*

NUMBERS
Dale A. Brueggemann, *Assemblies of God, Division of Foreign Missions*
Roland K. Harrison (deceased), *Wycliffe College*
Gerald L. Mattingly, *Johnson Bible College*

DEUTERONOMY
J. Gordon McConville, *The Cheltenham and Gloucester College of
  Higher Education*
Eugene H. Merrill, *Dallas Theological Seminary*
John A. Thompson, *University of Melbourne*

HISTORICAL BOOKS
Barry J. Beitzel, *General Reviewer*
Trinity Evangelical Divinity School

JOSHUA/JUDGES
Carl E. Armerding, *Schloss Mittersill Study Centre*
Barry J. Beitzel, *Trinity Evangelical Divinity School*
Lawson Stone, *Asbury Theological Seminary*

1 & 2 SAMUEL
Barry J. Beitzel, *Trinity Evangelical Divinity School*
V. Philips Long, *Covenant Theological Seminary*
J. Robert Vannoy, *Biblical Theological Seminary*

1 & 2 KINGS
Bill T. Arnold, *Asbury Theological Seminary*
William H. Barnes, *Southeastern College of the Assemblies of God*
Frederic W. Bush, *Fuller Theological Seminary*

1 & 2 CHRONICLES
Raymond B. Dillard (deceased), *Westminster Theological Seminary*
David A. Dorsey, *Evangelical School of Theology*
Terry Eves, *Calvin College*

EZRA/NEHEMIAH/ESTHER/RUTH
William C. Williams, *Southern California College*
Hugh G. M. Williamson, *Oxford University*

POETRY
Tremper Longman III, *General Reviewer*
Westminster Theological Seminary

JOB
August Konkel, *Providence Theological Seminary*
Tremper Longman III, *Westminster Theological Seminary*
Al Wolters, *Redeemer College*

PSALMS 1–75
Mark D. Futato, *Westminster Theological Seminary in California*
Douglas Green, *Westminster Theological Seminary*
Richard Pratt, *Reformed Theological Seminary*

PSALMS 76–150
David M. Howard Jr., *Trinity Evangelical Divinity School*
Raymond C. Ortlund Jr., *Trinity Evangelical Divinity School*
Willem VanGemeren, *Trinity Evangelical Divinity School*

PROVERBS
Ted Hildebrandt, *Grace College*
Richard Schultz, *Wheaton College*
Raymond C. Van Leeuwen, *Eastern College*

ECCLESIASTES/SONG OF SONGS
Daniel C. Fredericks, *Belhaven College*
David Hubbard, *Fuller Theological Seminary*
Tremper Longman III, *Westminster Theological Seminary*

PROPHETS
John N. Oswalt, *General Reviewer*
Asbury Theological Seminary

ISAIAH
John N. Oswalt, *Asbury Theological Seminary*
Gary Smith, *Bethel Theological Seminary*
John Walton, *Moody Bible Institute*

JEREMIAH/LAMENTATIONS
G. Herbert Livingston, *Asbury Theological Seminary*
Elmer A. Martens, *Mennonite Brethren Biblical Seminary*

EZEKIEL
Daniel I. Block, *The Southern Baptist Theological Seminary*
David H. Engelhard, *Calvin Theological Seminary*
David Thompson, *Asbury Theological Seminary*

DANIEL/HAGGAI/ZECHARIAH/MALACHI
Joyce Baldwin Caine (deceased), *Trinity College, Bristol*
Douglas Gropp, *Catholic University of America*
Roy Hayden, *Oral Roberts School of Theology*

HOSEA–ZEPHANIAH
Joseph Coleson, *Nazarene Theological Seminary*
Andrew Hill, *Wheaton College*
Richard Patterson, *Professor Emeritus, Liberty University*

GOSPELS AND ACTS
Grant R. Osborne, *General Reviewer*
Trinity Evangelical Divinity School

MATTHEW
Craig Blomberg, *Denver Conservative Baptist Seminary*
Donald A. Hagner, *Fuller Theological Seminary*
David Turner, *Grand Rapids Baptist Seminary*

MARK
Robert Guelich (deceased), *Fuller Theological Seminary*
Grant R. Osborne, *Trinity Evangelical Divinity School*

LUKE
Darrel Bock, *Dallas Theological Seminary*
Scot McKnight, *North Park College*
Robert Stein, *Bethel Theological Seminary*

JOHN
Gary M. Burge, *Wheaton College*
Philip W. Comfort, *Wheaton College*
Marianne Meye Thompson, *Fuller Theological Seminary*

ACTS
D. A. Carson, *Trinity Evangelical Divinity School*
William J. Larkin, *Columbia Biblical Seminary*
Roger Mohrlang, *Whitworth College*

LETTERS AND REVELATION
Norman R. Ericson, *General Reviewer*
Wheaton College

ROMANS/GALATIANS
Gerald Borchert, *The Southern Baptist Theological Seminary*
Douglas J. Moo, *Trinity Evangelical Divinity School*
Thomas R. Schreiner, *Bethel Theological Seminary*

1 & 2 CORINTHIANS
Joseph Alexanian, *Trinity International University*
Linda Belleville, *North Park Theological Seminary*
Douglas A. Oss, *Central Bible College*
Robert Sloan, *Baylor University*

EPHESIANS–PHILEMON
Harold W. Hoehner, *Dallas Theological Seminary*
Moises Silva, *Gordon-Conwell Theological Seminary*
Klyne Snodgrass, *North Park Theological Seminary*

HEBREWS/JAMES/1 & 2 PETER/JUDE
Peter Davids, *Canadian Theological Seminary*
Norman R. Ericson, *Wheaton College*
William Lane, *Seattle Pacific University*
J. Ramsey Michaels, *S.W. Missouri State University*

1–3 JOHN/REVELATION
Greg Beale, *Gordon-Conwell Theological Seminary*
Robert Mounce, *Whitworth College*
M. Robert Mulholland Jr., *Asbury Theological Seminary*

SPECIAL REVIEWERS
   F. F. Bruce (deceased), *University of Manchester*
   Kenneth N. Taylor, *Tyndale House Publishers*

COORDINATING TEAM
   Mark R. Norton, *Managing Editor and O.T. Coordinating Editor*
   Philip W. Comfort, *N.T. Coordinating Editor*
   Ronald A. Beers, *Executive Director and Stylist*
   Mark D. Taylor, *Director and Chief Stylist*

DAY 1

God's Good Creation
Genesis 1:1–2:4a

In the beginning God created* the heavens and the earth. ²The earth was empty, a formless mass cloaked in darkness. And the Spirit of God was hovering over its surface. ³Then God said, "Let there be light," and there was light. ⁴And God saw that it was good. Then he separated the light from the darkness. ⁵God called the light "day" and the darkness "night." Together these made up one day.

⁶And God said, "Let there be space between the waters, to separate water from water." ⁷And so it was. God made this space to separate the waters above from the waters below. ⁸And God called the space "sky." This happened on the second day.

⁹And God said, "Let the waters beneath the sky be

1:1 Or *In the beginning when God created,* or *When God began to create.*

gathered into one place so dry ground may appear." And so it was. [10]God named the dry ground "land" and the water "seas." And God saw that it was good. [11]Then God said, "Let the land burst forth with every sort of grass and seed-bearing plant. And let there be trees that grow seed-bearing fruit. The seeds will then produce the kinds of plants and trees from which they came." And so it was. [12]The land was filled with seed-bearing plants and trees, and their seeds produced plants and trees of like kind. And God saw that it was good. [13]This all happened on the third day.

[14]And God said, "Let bright lights appear in the sky to separate the day from the night. They will be signs to mark off the seasons, the days, and the years. [15]Let their light shine down upon the earth." And so it was. [16]For God made two great lights, the sun and the moon, to shine down upon the earth. The greater one, the sun, presides during the day; the lesser one, the moon, presides through the night. He also made the stars. [17]God set these lights in the heavens to light the earth, [18]to govern the day and the night, and to separate the light from the darkness. And God saw that it was good. [19]This all happened on the fourth day.

[20]And God said, "Let the waters swarm with fish and other life. Let the skies be filled with birds of every kind." [21]So God created great sea creatures and every sort of fish and every kind of bird. And God saw that it was good. [22]Then God blessed them, saying, "Let the fish multiply and fill the oceans. Let

the birds increase and fill the earth." ²³This all happened on the fifth day.

²⁴And God said, "Let the earth bring forth every kind of animal—livestock, small animals, and wildlife." And so it was. ²⁵God made all sorts of wild animals, livestock, and small animals, each able to reproduce more of its own kind. And God saw that it was good.

²⁶Then God said, "Let us make people* in our image, to be like ourselves. They will be masters over all life— the fish in the sea, the birds in the sky, and all the livestock, wild animals,* and small animals."

²⁷ So God created people in his own image;
    God patterned them after himself;
    male and female he created them.

²⁸God blessed them and told them, "Multiply and fill the earth and subdue it. Be masters over the fish and birds and all the animals." ²⁹And God said, "Look! I have given you the seed-bearing plants throughout the earth and all the fruit trees for your food. ³⁰And I have given all the grasses and other green plants to the animals and birds for their food." And so it was. ³¹Then God looked over all he had made, and he saw that it was excellent in every way. This all happened on the sixth day.

2 So the creation of the heavens and the earth and everything in them was completed. ²On the seventh day, having finished his task, God rested from all his

1:26a Hebrew *man*; also in 1:27.   1:26b As in Syriac version; Hebrew reads *all the earth.*

work. ³And God blessed the seventh day and declared it holy, because it was the day when he rested from his work of creation.

⁴This is the account of the creation of the heavens and the earth.

Thought for the Day

God, who embodies all that is splendid, glorious, and majestic, created a world that has those qualities. The marks of God's character are in God's creation; the excellence of creation is merely an extension of the excellence of the Creator himself. If we are to develop excellence in our lives, we should know intimately the one who is excellent. As we model our lives after the God of creativity, beauty, wisdom, and high standards, we will see our own lives and works reflecting those qualities.

DAY 2

A Call for Wholehearted Commitment
Deuteronomy 6:4-19

⁴"Hear, O Israel! The Lord is our God, the Lord alone.*
⁵And you must love the Lord your God with all your heart, all your soul, and all your strength. ⁶And you must commit yourselves wholeheartedly to these commands I am giving you today. ⁷Repeat them again and again to your children. Talk about them when you are at home and when you are away on a journey, when you

6:4 Or *The Lord our God is one Lord,* or *The Lord our God, the Lord is one,* or *The Lord is our God, the Lord is one.*

are lying down and when you are getting up again. [8]Tie them to your hands as a reminder, and wear them on your forehead. [9]Write them on the doorposts of your house and on your gates.

[10]"The LORD your God will soon bring you into the land he swore to give your ancestors Abraham, Isaac, and Jacob. It is a land filled with large, prosperous cities that you did not build. [11]The houses will be richly stocked with goods you did not produce. You will draw water from cisterns you did not dig, and you will eat from vineyards and olive trees you did not plant. When you have eaten your fill in this land, [12]be careful not to forget the LORD, who rescued you from slavery in the land of Egypt. [13]You must fear the LORD your God and serve him. When you take an oath, you must use only his name.

[14]"You must not worship any of the gods of neighboring nations, [15]for the LORD your God, who lives among you, is a jealous God. His anger will flare up against you and wipe you from the face of the earth. [16]Do not test the LORD your God as you did when you complained at Massah. [17]You must diligently obey the commands of the LORD your God—all the stipulations and laws he has given you. [18]Do what is right and good in the LORD's sight, so all will go well with you. Then you will enter and occupy the good land that the LORD solemnly promised to give your ancestors. [19]You will drive out all the enemies living in your land, just as the LORD said you would."

Thought for the Day

The word used for love in verse 5 primarily speaks of an act of mind and will. It is the Hebrew equivalent of the New Testament word for love, agape, which speaks of a committed, dedicated love.

Speaking of this commandment, Jesus said it "is the first and greatest commandment" (Matthew 22:37-38). In other words, if you love God with all of your heart, with all of your soul, and with all of your strength, the rest of the commandments will come naturally.

Love for God is the basis for all obedience. If you have an all-consuming love for God, you will want to do what pleases him. Make a commitment today to truly love God—not with some transient, shallow emotion, but with a wholehearted, sincere devotion. Place this holy and noble pursuit at the forefront of your life, and everything else will fall into place.

DAY 3

Choosing the Better Way
Joshua 24:14-27

[14]"So honor the LORD and serve him wholeheartedly. Put away forever the idols your ancestors worshiped when they lived beyond the Euphrates River and in Egypt. Serve the LORD alone. [15]But if you are unwilling to serve the LORD, then choose today whom you will serve. Would you prefer the gods your ancestors served beyond the Euphrates? Or will

it be the gods of the Amorites in whose land you now live? But as for me and my family, we will serve the LORD."

[16]The people replied, "We would never forsake the LORD and worship other gods. [17]For the LORD our God is the one who rescued us and our ancestors from slavery in the land of Egypt. He performed mighty miracles before our very eyes. As we traveled through the wilderness among our enemies, he preserved us. [18]It was the LORD who drove out the Amorites and the other nations living here in the land. So we, too, will serve the LORD, for he alone is our God."

[19]Then Joshua said to the people, "You are not able to serve the LORD, for he is a holy and jealous God. He will not forgive your rebellion and sins. [20]If you forsake the LORD and serve other gods, he will turn against you and destroy you, even though he has been so good to you."

[21]But the people answered Joshua, saying, "No, we are determined to serve the LORD!"

[22]"You are accountable for this decision," Joshua said. "You have chosen to serve the LORD."

"Yes," they replied, "we are accountable."

[23]"All right then," Joshua said, "destroy the idols among you, and turn your hearts to the LORD, the God of Israel."

[24]The people said to Joshua, "We will serve the LORD our God. We will obey him alone."

[25]So Joshua made a covenant with the people that

day at Shechem, committing them to a permanent and binding contract between themselves and the LORD. ²⁶Joshua recorded these things in the Book of the Law of God. As a reminder of their agreement, he took a huge stone and rolled it beneath the oak tree beside the Tabernacle of the LORD.

²⁷Joshua said to all the people, "This stone has heard everything the LORD said to us. It will be a witness to testify against you if you go back on your word to God."

Thought for the Day

Joshua told the Israelites to throw away their foreign gods, or idols. To follow God requires destroying whatever gets in the way of worshiping him. We have our own form of idols—greed, wrong priorities, jealousies, prejudices—that get in the way of worshiping God. God is not satisfied if we merely hide these idols. We must completely remove them from our lives.

DAY 4

God Is in Control
1 Kings 18:20-40

²⁰So Ahab summoned all the people and the prophets to Mount Carmel. ²¹Then Elijah stood in front of them and said, "How long are you going to waver between two opinions? If the LORD is God, follow him! But if Baal is God, then follow him!" But the people were completely silent.

²²Then Elijah said to them, "I am the only prophet of the LORD who is left, but Baal has 450 prophets. ²³Now bring two bulls. The prophets of Baal may choose whichever one they wish and cut it into pieces and lay it on the wood of their altar, but without setting fire to it. I will prepare the other bull and lay it on the wood on the altar, but not set fire to it. ²⁴Then call on the name of your god, and I will call on the name of the LORD. The god who answers by setting fire to the wood is the true God!" And all the people agreed.

²⁵Then Elijah said to the prophets of Baal, "You go first, for there are many of you. Choose one of the bulls and prepare it and call on the name of your god. But do not set fire to the wood."

²⁶So they prepared one of the bulls and placed it on the altar. Then they called on the name of Baal all morning, shouting, "O Baal, answer us!" But there was no reply of any kind. Then they danced wildly around the altar they had made.

²⁷About noontime Elijah began mocking them. "You'll have to shout louder," he scoffed, "for surely he is a god! Perhaps he is deep in thought, or he is relieving himself. Or maybe he is away on a trip, or he is asleep and needs to be wakened!"

²⁸So they shouted louder, and following their normal custom, they cut themselves with knives and swords until the blood gushed out. ²⁹They raved all afternoon until the time of the evening sacrifice, but still there was no reply, no voice, no answer.

³⁰Then Elijah called to the people, "Come over here!" They all crowded around him as he repaired the altar of the LORD that had been torn down. ³¹He took twelve stones, one to represent each of the tribes of Israel,* ³²and he used the stones to rebuild the LORD's altar. Then he dug a trench around the altar large enough to hold about three gallons.* ³³He piled wood on the altar, cut the bull into pieces, and laid the pieces on the wood. Then he said, "Fill four large jars with water, and pour the water over the offering and the wood." After they had done this, ³⁴he said, "Do the same thing again!" And when they were finished, he said, "Now do it a third time!" So they did as he said, ³⁵and the water ran around the altar and even overflowed the trench.

³⁶At the customary time for offering the evening sacrifice, Elijah the prophet walked up to the altar and prayed, "O LORD, God of Abraham, Isaac, and Jacob,* prove today that you are God in Israel and that I am your servant. Prove that I have done all this at your command. ³⁷O LORD, answer me! Answer me so these people will know that you, O LORD, are God and that you have brought them back to yourself."

³⁸Immediately the fire of the LORD flashed down from heaven and burned up the young bull, the wood, the stones, and the dust. It even licked up all the water in the ditch! ³⁹And when the people saw it,

18:31 Hebrew *each of the tribes of the sons of Jacob to whom the LORD had said, "Your name will be Israel."* 18:32 Hebrew *2 seahs [12 liters] of seed.* 18:36 Hebrew *and Israel.*

they fell on their faces and cried out, "The LORD is God! The LORD is God!"

⁴⁰Then Elijah commanded, "Seize all the prophets of Baal. Don't let a single one escape!" So the people seized them all, and Elijah took them down to the Kishon Valley and killed them there.

Thought for the Day

God flashed fire from heaven for Elijah, and he will help us accomplish what he commands us to do. The proof may not be as dramatic in our lives as in Elijah's, but God will make resources available to us in creative ways to accomplish his purposes. He will give us the wisdom to raise a family, the courage to take a stand for truth, or the means to provide help for someone in need. Like Elijah, we can have faith that whatever God commands us to do, he will provide what we need to carry it through.

DAY 5

The Choice Is Yours
Psalm 1:1-6

¹ Oh, the joys of those
    who do not follow the advice of the wicked,
    or stand around with sinners,
    or join in with scoffers.
² But they delight in doing everything the LORD
    wants;
    day and night they think about his law.

³ They are like trees planted along the riverbank,
   bearing fruit each season without fail.
  Their leaves never wither,
   and in all they do, they prosper.

⁴ But this is not true of the wicked.
   They are like worthless chaff, scattered by the
   wind.
⁵ They will be condemned at the time of
   judgment.
   Sinners will have no place among the godly.

⁶ For the LORD watches over the path of the
   godly,
   but the path of the wicked leads to
   destruction.

Thought for the Day
   The intimacy of any relationship is a function of
both the amount of time spent together and the quality
of what is accomplished or shared in that time. If a
parent and child spend three hours together, but those
hours are spent watching television, the time doesn't
establish intimacy. This psalm suggests that an
intimate relationship with God grows out of both the
quantity and the quality of time we spend focused on
him. Do you intentionally and consistently spend time
alone with God?

DAY 6

The Majesty of the LORD
Psalm 8:1-9

For the choir director: A psalm of David, to be accompanied by a stringed instrument. *

1 O LORD, our Lord, the majesty of your name fills
    the earth!
    Your glory is higher than the heavens.

2 You have taught children and nursing infants
    to give you praise.*
  They silence your enemies
    who were seeking revenge.

3 When I look at the night sky and see the work of
    your fingers—
    the moon and the stars you have set in place—

4 what are mortals that you should think of us,
    mere humans that you should care for us?*

5 For you made us only a little lower than God,*
    and you crowned us with glory and honor.

6 You put us in charge of everything you made,
    giving us authority over all things—

7 the sheep and the cattle
    and all the wild animals,

8 the birds in the sky, the fish in the sea,
    and everything that swims the ocean currents.

8:TITLE Hebrew *according to the gittith.* 8:2 As in Greek version; Hebrew reads *to show strength.* 8:4 Hebrew *what is man that you should think of him, the son of man that you should care for him?* 8:5 Or *a little lower than the angels;* Hebrew reads *Elohim.*

13

⁹ O LORD, our Lord, the majesty of your name fills
the earth!

Thought for the Day

*The psalmist could not understand how the God
who made the stars could have any interest in a mere
human being. This is healthy humility. Then the
psalmist caught a glimpse of God's perspective: We
were made just a little lower than God himself. When
we recognize that God bestows on us this kind of honor
and glory, we begin to understand our value. The
healthiest self-image is produced from the merging of
humility and God-given honor. We dishonor God when
we dishonor ourselves; we also dishonor God when we
forget that our life and position come from him.*

DAY 7

Make Me Clean
Psalm 51:1-19

*For the choir director: A psalm of David, regarding the
time Nathan the prophet came to him after David had
committed adultery with Bathsheba.*

¹ Have mercy on me, O God,
    because of your unfailing love.
  Because of your great compassion,
    blot out the stain of my sins.
² Wash me clean from my guilt.
    Purify me from my sin.

³ For I recognize my shameful deeds—
   they haunt me day and night.
⁴ Against you, and you alone, have I sinned;
   I have done what is evil in your sight.
   You will be proved right in what you say,
   and your judgment against me is just.

⁵ For I was born a sinner—
   yes, from the moment my mother conceived me.
⁶ But you desire honesty from the heart,
   so you can teach me to be wise in my inmost being.

⁷ Purify me from my sins,* and I will be clean;
   wash me, and I will be whiter than snow.
⁸ Oh, give me back my joy again;
   you have broken me—
   now let me rejoice.
⁹ Don't keep looking at my sins.
   Remove the stain of my guilt.
¹⁰ Create in me a clean heart, O God.
   Renew a right spirit within me.
¹¹ Do not banish me from your presence,
   and don't take your Holy Spirit from me.
¹² Restore to me again the joy of your salvation,
   and make me willing to obey you.
¹³ Then I will teach your ways to sinners,
   and they will return to you.
¹⁴ Forgive me for shedding blood, O God who saves;
   then I will joyfully sing of your forgiveness.

51:7 Hebrew *Purify me with the hyssop branch.*

^{15} Unseal my lips, O Lord,
  that I may praise you.

^{16} You would not be pleased with sacrifices,
  or I would bring them.
 If I brought you a burnt offering,
  you would not accept it.
^{17} The sacrifice you want is a broken spirit.
  A broken and repentant heart, O God,
  you will not despise.

^{18} Look with favor on Zion and help her;
  rebuild the walls of Jerusalem.
^{19} Then you will be pleased with worthy sacrifices
  and with our whole burnt offerings;
  and bulls will again be sacrificed on your altar.

Thought for the Day

Because we are born as sinners (verse 5), our natural inclination is to please ourselves rather than God. David followed that inclination when he took another man's wife. We also follow it when we sin in any way. Like David, we must ask God to purify us from within (verse 10), clearing our hearts and spirits for new thoughts and desires. Right conduct can come only from a clean heart and spirit. Ask God to create a pure heart and spirit in you.

DAY 8

Trusting in the LORD
Proverbs 3:1-18

My child,* never forget the things I have taught you. Store my commands in your heart, ²for they will give you a long and satisfying life. ³Never let loyalty and kindness get away from you! Wear them like a necklace; write them deep within your heart. ⁴Then you will find favor with both God and people, and you will gain a good reputation.

⁵Trust in the LORD with all your heart; do not depend on your own understanding. ⁶Seek his will in all you do, and he will direct your paths.

⁷Don't be impressed with your own wisdom. Instead, fear the LORD and turn your back on evil. ⁸Then you will gain renewed health and vitality.

⁹Honor the LORD with your wealth and with the best part of everything your land produces. ¹⁰Then he will fill your barns with grain, and your vats will overflow with the finest wine.

¹¹My child, don't ignore it when the LORD disciplines you, and don't be discouraged when he corrects you. ¹²For the LORD corrects those he loves, just as a father corrects a child* in whom he delights.

¹³Happy is the person who finds wisdom and gains understanding. ¹⁴For the profit of wisdom is better than silver, and her wages are better than gold. ¹⁵Wisdom is

3:1 Hebrew *My son*; also in 3:11, 21. **3:12** Hebrew *a son*.

more precious than rubies; nothing you desire can compare with her. [16]She offers you life in her right hand, and riches and honor in her left. [17]She will guide you down delightful paths; all her ways are satisfying. [18]Wisdom is a tree of life to those who embrace her; happy are those who hold her tightly.

Thought for the Day

One of the most difficult things for us to do as human beings is to fully entrust something to someone. We have an inherent desire to be in control, to make our own plans and decisions. Yet, verses 5 and 6 fly in the face of that philosophy. To find God's will, you need to completely trust God and his judgment and timing. How do you practically do this in your life? Always ask God for his will to supersede your own in your prayers. Seek God before you start making decisions, not afterward. Spend time looking for what God's Word has to say about a certain decision. Honor God by turning your back on evil.

To "put God first" is the same principle Jesus gave us in Matthew 6:33, where he reminded us to "make the Kingdom of God [our] primary concern." This simply means that we consider his will as revealed in Scripture as we grapple with the decisions of life. Not only will you find his will in this process, but you also will "gain renewed health and vitality" (verse 8). Remember this passage of Scripture whenever you are faced with a moment of decision or uncertainty. You can rest assured, knowing that God wants to be an

*integral part of every decision you make and every
step you take.*

DAY 9

A Wife of Noble Character
Proverbs 31:10-31

[10]Who can find a virtuous and capable wife? She is worth more than precious rubies. [11]Her husband can trust her, and she will greatly enrich his life. [12]She will not hinder him but help him all her life.

[13]She finds wool and flax and busily spins it. [14]She is like a merchant's ship; she brings her food from afar. [15]She gets up before dawn to prepare breakfast for her household and plan the day's work for her servant girls. [16]She goes out to inspect a field and buys it; with her earnings she plants a vineyard.

[17]She is energetic and strong, a hard worker. [18]She watches for bargains; her lights burn late into the night. [19]Her hands are busy spinning thread, her fingers twisting fiber.

[20]She extends a helping hand to the poor and opens her arms to the needy.

[21]She has no fear of winter for her household because all of them have warm* clothes. [22]She quilts her own bedspreads. She dresses like royalty in gowns of finest cloth.

[23]Her husband is well known, for he sits in the council meeting with the other civic leaders.

31:21 As in Greek version; Hebrew *scarlet*.

²⁴She makes belted linen garments and sashes to sell to the merchants.

²⁵She is clothed with strength and dignity, and she laughs with no fear of the future. ²⁶When she speaks, her words are wise, and kindness is the rule when she gives instructions. ²⁷She carefully watches all that goes on in her household and does not have to bear the consequences of laziness.

²⁸Her children stand and bless her. Her husband praises her: ²⁹"There are many virtuous and capable women in the world, but you surpass them all!"

³⁰Charm is deceptive, and beauty does not last; but a woman who fears the LORD will be greatly praised. ³¹Reward her for all she has done. Let her deeds publicly declare her praise.

Thought for the Day

In our society where physical appearance counts for so much, it may surprise some that the appearance of this woman is never mentioned. Her attractiveness comes entirely from her character, which is the subject of the author's praise. This woman is a loving wife and mother. She is industrious, wise, and compassionate. She considers the needs of others more important than her own. But most important, she fears the Lord. In her example, we see what is beautiful to the Lord—a good character—and we are challenged to improve what cannot be seen.

DAY 10

A Time for Everything
Ecclesiastes 3:1-15

1 There is a time for everything,
a season for every activity under heaven.
2 A time to be born and a time to die.
A time to plant and a time to harvest.
3 A time to kill and a time to heal.
A time to tear down and a time to rebuild.
4 A time to cry and a time to laugh.
A time to grieve and a time to dance.
5 A time to scatter stones and a time to gather
stones.
A time to embrace and a time to turn away.
6 A time to search and a time to lose.
A time to keep and a time to throw away.
7 A time to tear and a time to mend.
A time to be quiet and a time to speak up.
8 A time to love and a time to hate.
A time for war and a time for peace.

9What do people really get for all their hard work?
10I have thought about this in connection with the
various kinds of work God has given people to do.
11God has made everything beautiful for its own time.
He has planted eternity in the human heart, but even
so, people cannot see the whole scope of God's work
from beginning to end. 12So I concluded that there is
nothing better for people than to be happy and to

enjoy themselves as long as they can. [13]And people should eat and drink and enjoy the fruits of their labor, for these are gifts from God.

[14]And I know that whatever God does is final. Nothing can be added to it or taken from it. God's purpose in this is that people should fear him. [15]Whatever exists today and whatever will exist in the future has already existed in the past. For God calls each event back in its turn.*

Thought for the Day

What is the purpose of life? It is that we should fear the all-powerful God. To fear God means to respect and stand in awe of him because of who he is. Purpose in life starts with whom we know, not what we know or how good we are. It is impossible to fulfill your God-given purpose unless you revere God and give him first place in your life.

DAY 11

Comfort for God's People
Isaiah 40:1-11, 27-31

"Comfort, comfort my people," says your God. [2]"Speak tenderly to Jerusalem. Tell her that her sad days are gone and that her sins are pardoned. Yes, the LORD has punished her in full for all her sins."

[3]Listen! I hear the voice of someone shouting, "Make a highway for the LORD through the wilderness. Make a

3:15 Hebrew *For God calls the past to account.*

22

straight, smooth road through the desert for our God. 4Fill the valleys and level the hills. Straighten out the curves and smooth off the rough spots. 5Then the glory of the LORD will be revealed, and all people will see it together. The LORD has spoken!"

6A voice said, "Shout!"

I asked, "What should I shout?"

"Shout that people are like the grass that dies away. Their beauty fades as quickly as the beauty of flowers in a field. 7The grass withers, and the flowers fade beneath the breath of the LORD. And so it is with people. 8The grass withers, and the flowers fade, but the word of our God stands forever."

9Messenger of good news, shout to Zion from the mountaintops! Shout louder to Jerusalem—do not be afraid. Tell the towns of Judah, "Your God is coming!" 10Yes, the Sovereign LORD is coming in all his glorious power. He will rule with awesome strength. See, he brings his reward with him as he comes. 11He will feed his flock like a shepherd. He will carry the lambs in his arms, holding them close to his heart. He will gently lead the mother sheep with their young. . . .

27O Israel, how can you say the LORD does not see your troubles? How can you say God refuses to hear your case? 28Have you never heard or understood? Don't you know that the LORD is the everlasting God, the Creator of all the earth? He never grows faint or weary. No one can measure the depths of his understanding. 29He gives power to those who are tired and worn out; he offers strength to the weak. ³⁰Even youths will become exhausted, and young men will give up. ³¹But those who wait on the LORD will find new strength. They will fly high on wings like eagles. They will run and not grow weary. They will walk and not faint.

Thought for the Day

Even the strongest people get tired at times, but God's power and strength never diminish. He is never too tired or too busy to help and listen. His strength is our source of strength. When you feel all of life crushing you, and you cannot go another step, remember that you can call upon God to renew your strength.

DAY 12

Victory through Suffering
Isaiah 52:13–53:12

¹³See, my servant will prosper; he will be highly exalted. ¹⁴Many were amazed when they saw him*—beaten and bloodied, so disfigured one would scarcely know he was a person. ¹⁵And he will again startle* many nations. Kings will stand speechless in his presence. For they will see what they had not previously been told about; they will understand what they had not heard about.

53 Who has believed our message? To whom will the LORD reveal his saving power? ²My servant grew up in the LORD's presence like a tender green shoot, sprouting

52:14 As in Syriac version; Hebrew reads *you*. 52:15 Or *cleanse.*

from a root in dry and sterile ground. There was nothing beautiful or majestic about his appearance, nothing to attract us to him. ³He was despised and rejected—a man of sorrows, acquainted with bitterest grief. We turned our backs on him and looked the other way when he went by. He was despised, and we did not care.

⁴Yet it was our weaknesses he carried; it was our sorrows* that weighed him down. And we thought his troubles were a punishment from God for his own sins! ⁵But he was wounded and crushed for our sins. He was beaten that we might have peace. He was whipped, and we were healed! ⁶All of us have strayed away like sheep. We have left God's paths to follow our own. Yet the LORD laid on him the guilt and sins of us all.

⁷He was oppressed and treated harshly, yet he never said a word. He was led as a lamb to the slaughter. And as a sheep is silent before the shearers, he did not open his mouth. ⁸From prison and trial they led him away to his death. But who among the people realized that he was dying for their sins—that he was suffering their punishment? ⁹He had done no wrong, and he never deceived anyone. But he was buried like a criminal; he was put in a rich man's grave.

¹⁰But it was the LORD's good plan to crush him and fill him with grief. Yet when his life is made an offering for sin, he will have a multitude of children, many heirs. He will enjoy a long life, and the LORD's plan will prosper in his hands. ¹¹When he sees all that is accomplished by his

53:4 Or *Yet it was our sicknesses he carried; it was our diseases.*

anguish, he will be satisfied. And because of what he has experienced, my righteous servant will make it possible for many to be counted righteous, for he will bear all their sins. ¹²I will give him the honors of one who is mighty and great, because he exposed himself to death. He was counted among those who were sinners. He bore the sins of many and interceded for sinners.

Thought for the Day

Most of us experience painful rejection sometime in our lives. It may be the loneliness of relational failure, the esteem-shattering experience of job termination, or the self-condemnation of a guilty conscience. Since we feel rejected by others and sometimes reject ourselves, we often assume that God rejects us as well. In this passage, the prophet anticipates the rejection Jesus would suffer on our behalf. Christ knows not only all the rejection of human life but also the rejection and pain of the cross itself. We can take great hope and comfort in knowing that Jesus understands and feels our rejection. He went to the cross so that we could always know the acceptance and love of God.

DAY 13

God's Unfailing Love
Hosea 11:1-11

"When Israel was a child, I loved him as a son, and I called my son out of Egypt. ²But the more I* called to

11:2 As in Greek version; Hebrew reads *they.*

him, the more he rebelled, offering sacrifices to the images of Baal and burning incense to idols. ³It was I who taught Israel* how to walk, leading him along by the hand. But he doesn't know or even care that it was I who took care of him. ⁴I led Israel along with my ropes of kindness and love. I lifted the yoke from his neck, and I myself stooped to feed him.

⁵"But since my people refuse to return to me, they will go back to Egypt and will be forced to serve Assyria. ⁶War will swirl through their cities; their enemies will crash through their gates and destroy them, trapping them in their own evil plans. ⁷For my people are determined to desert me. They call me the Most High, but they don't truly honor me.

⁸"Oh, how can I give you up, Israel? How can I let you go? How can I destroy you like Admah and Zeboiim? My heart is torn within me, and my compassion overflows. ⁹No, I will not punish you as much as my burning anger tells me to. I will not completely destroy Israel, for I am God and not a mere mortal. I am the Holy One living among you, and I will not come to destroy.

¹⁰"For someday the people will follow the LORD. I will roar like a lion, and my people will return trembling from the west. ¹¹Like a flock of birds, they will come from Egypt. Flying like doves, they will return from Assyria. And I will bring them home again," says the LORD.

11:3 Hebrew *Ephraim,* referring to the northern kingdom of Israel; also in 11:8, 9, 12.

Thought for the Day

God's discipline requires times of leading and times of feeding. Sometimes the rope is taut; sometimes it is slack. God's discipline is always loving, and its object is always the well-being of the beloved. When you are called to discipline others—children, students, employees, or church members—do not be rigid. Vary your approach according to the goals you are seeking to accomplish. In each case, ask yourself, "Does this person need guidance, or does he or she need to be nurtured?"

DAY 14

A Promise of Renewal
Malachi 4:1-6

The LORD Almighty says, "The day of judgment is coming, burning like a furnace. The arrogant and the wicked will be burned up like straw on that day. They will be consumed like a tree—roots and all.

² "But for you who fear my name, the Sun of Righteousness will rise with healing in his wings.* And you will go free, leaping with joy like calves let out to pasture. ³ On the day when I act, you will tread upon the wicked as if they were dust under your feet," says the LORD Almighty.

⁴ "Remember to obey the instructions of my servant Moses, all the laws and regulations that I gave him on Mount Sinai* for all Israel.

4:2 Or *the sun of righteousness will rise with healing in its wings.* 4:4 Hebrew *Horeb*, another name for Sinai.

28

⁵"Look, I am sending you the prophet Elijah before the great and dreadful day of the LORD arrives. ⁶His preaching will turn the hearts of parents* to their children, and the hearts of children to their parents. Otherwise I will come and strike the land with a curse."

Thought for the Day

These last verses of the Old Testament are filled with hope. Regardless of how life looks now, God controls the future, and everything will be made right. We who have loved and served God look forward to a joyful celebration. This hope for the future becomes ours when we trust God with our lives.

DAY 15

Following Jesus' Example
Matthew 5:1-12

One day as the crowds were gathering, Jesus went up the mountainside with his disciples and sat down to teach them.

The Beatitudes

²This is what he taught them:

³ "God blesses those who realize their need for him,*
  for the Kingdom of Heaven is given to them.
⁴ God blesses those who mourn,
  for they will be comforted.

4:6 Hebrew *fathers;* also in 4:6b. 5:3 Greek *the poor in spirit.*

⁵ God blesses those who are gentle and lowly,
  for the whole earth will belong to them.
⁶ God blesses those who are hungry and thirsty for
    justice,
  for they will receive it in full.
⁷ God blesses those who are merciful,
  for they will be shown mercy.
⁸ God blesses those whose hearts are pure,
  for they will see God.
⁹ God blesses those who work for peace,
  for they will be called the children of God.
¹⁰ God blesses those who are persecuted because
    they live for God,
  for the Kingdom of Heaven is theirs.

¹¹"God blesses you when you are mocked and persecuted and lied about because you are my followers. ¹²Be happy about it! Be very glad! For a great reward awaits you in heaven. And remember, the ancient prophets were persecuted, too."

Thought for the Day

Each beatitude tells how to be blessed by God, which means more than being happy. It implies the fortunate or enviable state of those who are in God's Kingdom. The Beatitudes don't promise laughter, pleasure, or earthly prosperity. To Jesus, being "blessed" by God means the experience of hope and joy, independent of outward circumstances. To find hope and joy, the deepest form of happiness, follow Jesus no matter what the cost.

Christ's Miraculous Provision
Mark 6:30-44

³⁰The apostles returned to Jesus from their ministry tour and told him all they had done and what they had taught. ³¹Then Jesus said, "Let's get away from the crowds for a while and rest." There were so many people coming and going that Jesus and his apostles didn't even have time to eat. ³²They left by boat for a quieter spot. ³³But many people saw them leaving, and people from many towns ran ahead along the shore and met them as they landed. ³⁴A vast crowd was there as he stepped from the boat, and he had compassion on them because they were like sheep without a shepherd. So he taught them many things.

³⁵Late in the afternoon his disciples came to him and said, "This is a desolate place, and it is getting late. ³⁶Send the crowds away so they can go to the nearby farms and villages and buy themselves some food."

³⁷But Jesus said, "You feed them."

"With what?" they asked. "It would take a small fortune* to buy food for all this crowd!"

³⁸"How much food do you have?" he asked. "Go and find out."

They came back and reported, "We have five loaves of bread and two fish." ³⁹Then Jesus told the crowd to sit down in groups on the green grass. ⁴⁰So they sat in groups of fifty or a hundred.

6:37 Greek *200 denarii.* A denarius was the equivalent of a full day's wage.

[41]Jesus took the five loaves and two fish, looked up toward heaven, and asked God's blessing on the food. Breaking the loaves into pieces, he kept giving the bread and fish to the disciples to give to the people. [42]They all ate as much as they wanted, [43]and they picked up twelve baskets of leftover bread and fish. [44]Five thousand men had eaten from those five loaves!

Thought for the Day

When Jesus asked the disciples to provide food for more than 5,000 people, they asked in astonishment if they should go and spend a small fortune on bread. How do you react when you are given an impossible task? A situation that seems impossible with human resources is simply an opportunity for God. The disciples did everything they could by gathering the available food and organizing the people into groups. Then, in answer to prayer, God did the impossible. When facing a seemingly impossible task, do what you can and ask God to do the rest. He may see fit to make the impossible happen.

DAY 17

The Heart of a Servant
Luke 1:26-38

[26]In the sixth month of Elizabeth's pregnancy, God sent the angel Gabriel to Nazareth, a village in Galilee, [27]to a virgin named Mary. She was engaged to be married to a man named Joseph, a descendant of King

David. ²⁸Gabriel appeared to her and said, "Greetings, favored woman! The Lord is with you!*"

²⁹Confused and disturbed, Mary tried to think what the angel could mean. ³⁰"Don't be frightened, Mary," the angel told her, "for God has decided to bless you! ³¹You will become pregnant and have a son, and you are to name him Jesus. ³²He will be very great and will be called the Son of the Most High. And the Lord God will give him the throne of his ancestor David. ³³And he will reign over Israel* forever; his Kingdom will never end!"

³⁴Mary asked the angel, "But how can I have a baby? I am a virgin."

³⁵The angel replied, "The Holy Spirit will come upon you, and the power of the Most High will overshadow you. So the baby born to you will be holy, and he will be called the Son of God. ³⁶What's more, your relative Elizabeth has become pregnant in her old age! People used to say she was barren, but she's already in her sixth month. ³⁷For nothing is impossible with God."

³⁸Mary responded, "I am the Lord's servant, and I am willing to accept whatever he wants. May everything you have said come true." And then the angel left.

Thought for the Day

A young unmarried girl who became pregnant risked disaster. Unless the father of the child agreed to marry her, she would probably remain unmarried for life. If her own father rejected her, she could be forced into

1:28 Some manuscripts add *Blessed are you among women.* 1:33 Greek *over the house of Jacob.*

begging or prostitution in order to earn her living. And Mary, with her story about being made pregnant by the Holy Spirit, risked being considered crazy as well. Still Mary said, despite the possible risks, "May everything you have said come true." When Mary said that, she didn't know about the tremendous opportunity she would have. She only knew that God was asking her to serve him, and she willingly obeyed. Don't wait to see the bottom line before offering your life to God. Offer yourself willingly, even when the outcome seems disastrous.

DAY 18

Our Savior's Love for Us
John 1:1-18

In the beginning the Word already existed. He was with God, and he was God. ²He was in the beginning with God. ³He created everything there is. Nothing exists that he didn't make. ⁴Life itself was in him, and this life gives light to everyone. ⁵The light shines through the darkness, and the darkness can never extinguish it.

⁶God sent John the Baptist ⁷to tell everyone about the light so that everyone might believe because of his testimony. ⁸John himself was not the light; he was only a witness to the light. ⁹The one who is the true light, who gives light to everyone, was going to come into the world.

¹⁰But although the world was made through him, the world didn't recognize him when he came. ¹¹Even in his own land and among his own people, he was not accepted. ¹²But to all who believed him and accepted him, he gave the right to become children of God. ¹³They are reborn! This is not a physical birth resulting from human passion or plan—this rebirth comes from God.

¹⁴So the Word became human and lived here on earth among us. He was full of unfailing love and faithfulness.* And we have seen his glory, the glory of the only Son of the Father.

¹⁵John pointed him out to the people. He shouted to the crowds, "This is the one I was talking about when I said, 'Someone is coming who is far greater than I am, for he existed long before I did.'"

¹⁶We have all benefited from the rich blessings he brought to us—one gracious blessing after another.* ¹⁷For the law was given through Moses; God's unfailing love and faithfulness came through Jesus Christ. ¹⁸No one has ever seen God. But his only Son, who is himself God,* is near to the Father's heart; he has told us about him.

Thought for the Day

We, like John the Baptist, are not the source of God's light; we merely reflect that light. Jesus Christ is the true Light; he helps us see our way to God and shows us how

1:14 Greek *grace and truth;* also in 1:17. 1:16 Greek *grace upon grace.* 1:18 Some manuscripts read *his one and only Son.*

to walk along that way. But Christ has chosen to reflect his light through his followers to an unbelieving world, perhaps because unbelievers are not able to bear the full blazing glory of his light firsthand. The word witness indicates our role as reflectors of Christ's light. We are never to present ourselves as the light to others but are always to point them to Christ, the Light.

DAY 19

The Good Shepherd Cares for His Sheep
John 10:1-21

"I assure you, anyone who sneaks over the wall of a sheepfold, rather than going through the gate, must surely be a thief and a robber! ²For a shepherd enters through the gate. ³The gatekeeper opens the gate for him, and the sheep hear his voice and come to him. He calls his own sheep by name and leads them out. ⁴After he has gathered his own flock, he walks ahead of them, and they follow him because they recognize his voice. ⁵They won't follow a stranger; they will run from him because they don't recognize his voice."

⁶Those who heard Jesus use this illustration didn't understand what he meant, ⁷so he explained it to them. "I assure you, I am the gate for the sheep," he said. ⁸"All others who came before me were thieves and robbers. But the true sheep did not listen to them. ⁹Yes, I am the gate. Those who come in through me will be saved.

Wherever they go, they will find green pastures. [10]The thief's purpose is to steal and kill and destroy. My purpose is to give life in all its fullness.

[11]"I am the good shepherd. The good shepherd lays down his life for the sheep. [12]A hired hand will run when he sees a wolf coming. He will leave the sheep because they aren't his and he isn't their shepherd. And so the wolf attacks them and scatters the flock. [13]The hired hand runs away because he is merely hired and has no real concern for the sheep.

[14]"I am the good shepherd; I know my own sheep, and they know me, [15]just as my Father knows me and I know the Father. And I lay down my life for the sheep. [16]I have other sheep, too, that are not in this sheepfold. I must bring them also, and they will listen to my voice; and there will be one flock with one shepherd.

[17]"The Father loves me because I lay down my life that I may have it back again. [18]No one can take my life from me. I lay down my life voluntarily. For I have the right to lay it down when I want to and also the power to take it again. For my Father has given me this command."

[19]When he said these things, the people* were again divided in their opinions about him. [20]Some of them said, "He has a demon, or he's crazy. Why listen to a man like that?" [21]Others said, "This doesn't sound like a man possessed by a demon! Can a demon open the eyes of the blind?"

10:19 Greek *Jewish people.*

Thought for the Day

At night, sheep were often gathered into a sheepfold to protect them from thieves, weather, or wild animals. The sheepfolds were caves, sheds, or open areas surrounded by walls made of stones or branches. The shepherd often slept in the fold to protect the sheep. Just as a shepherd cares for his sheep, Jesus, the good shepherd, cares for his flock (those who follow him).

DAY 20

The Future Glory
Romans 8:28-39

²⁸And we know that God causes everything to work together* for the good of those who love God and are called according to his purpose for them. ²⁹For God knew his people in advance, and he chose them to become like his Son, so that his Son would be the firstborn, with many brothers and sisters. ³⁰And having chosen them, he called them to come to him. And he gave them right standing with himself, and he promised them his glory.

Nothing Can Separate Us from God's Love

³¹What can we say about such wonderful things as these? If God is for us, who can ever be against us? ³²Since God did not spare even his own Son but gave him up for us all, won't God, who gave us Christ, also give us everything else?

8:28 Some manuscripts read *And we know that everything works together.*

[33]Who dares accuse us whom God has chosen for his own? Will God? No! He is the one who has given us right standing with himself. [34]Who then will condemn us? Will Christ Jesus? No, for he is the one who died for us and was raised to life for us and is sitting at the place of highest honor next to God, pleading for us.

[35]Can anything ever separate us from Christ's love? Does it mean he no longer loves us if we have trouble or calamity, or are persecuted, or are hungry or cold or in danger or threatened with death? [36](Even the Scriptures say, "For your sake we are killed every day; we are being slaughtered like sheep."*) [37]No, despite all these things, overwhelming victory is ours through Christ, who loved us.

[38]And I am convinced that nothing can ever separate us from his love. Death can't, and life can't. The angels can't, and the demons can't. Our fears for today, our worries about tomorrow, and even the powers of hell can't keep God's love away. [39]Whether we are high above the sky or in the deepest ocean, nothing in all creation will ever be able to separate us from the love of God that is revealed in Christ Jesus our Lord.

Thought for the Day

These words were written to a church that would soon undergo terrible persecution. In just a few years, Paul's hypothetical situations would turn into painful

8:36 Ps 44:22.

realities. This passage reaffirms God's profound love for his people. No matter what happens to us, no matter where we are, we can never be separated from his love. Suffering should not drive us away from God, but help us to identify with him further and allow his love to reach us and heal us.

DAY 21

A Call to Love
1 Corinthians 13:1-13

If I could speak in any language in heaven or on earth* but didn't love others, I would only be making meaningless noise like a loud gong or a clanging cymbal. ²If I had the gift of prophecy, and if I knew all the mysteries of the future and knew everything about everything, but didn't love others, what good would I be? And if I had the gift of faith so that I could speak to a mountain and make it move, without love I would be no good to anybody. ³If I gave everything I have to the poor and even sacrificed my body, I could boast about it;* but if I didn't love others, I would be of no value whatsoever.

⁴Love is patient and kind. Love is not jealous or boastful or proud ⁵or rude. Love does not demand its own way. Love is not irritable, and it keeps no record of when it has been wronged. ⁶It is never glad about

13:1 Greek *in tongues of people and angels.* 13:3 Some manuscripts read *and even gave my body to be burned.*

injustice but rejoices whenever the truth wins out. [7]Love never gives up, never loses faith, is always hopeful, and endures through every circumstance.

[8]Love will last forever, but prophecy and speaking in unknown languages* and special knowledge will all disappear. [9]Now we know only a little, and even the gift of prophecy reveals little! [10]But when the end comes, these special gifts will all disappear.

[11]It's like this: When I was a child, I spoke and thought and reasoned as a child does. But when I grew up, I put away childish things. [12]Now we see things imperfectly as in a poor mirror, but then we will see everything with perfect clarity.* All that I know now is partial and incomplete, but then I will know everything completely, just as God knows me now.

[13]There are three things that will endure—faith, hope, and love—and the greatest of these is love.

Thought for the Day

The kind of love God wants us to give others is impossible to "manufacture" on our own. You might say that it is a "supernatural" love. It is a natural outflow of God's presence in our lives. That is why the Bible says, "[God] has given us the Holy Spirit to fill our hearts with his love" (Romans 5:5).

If you feel your love for others is falling short of God's ideal, ask the Holy Spirit to strengthen you in this area. Your relationships with others will never be the same.

13:8 Or *in tongues.* 13:12 Greek *see face to face.*

DAY 22

Christ's Power in Us
2 Corinthians 4:1-12

And so, since God in his mercy has given us this wonderful ministry, we never give up. ²We reject all shameful and underhanded methods. We do not try to trick anyone, and we do not distort the word of God. We tell the truth before God, and all who are honest know that.

³If the Good News we preach is veiled from anyone, it is a sign that they are perishing. ⁴Satan, the god of this evil world, has blinded the minds of those who don't believe, so they are unable to see the glorious light of the Good News that is shining upon them. They don't understand the message we preach about the glory of Christ, who is the exact likeness of God.

⁵We don't go around preaching about ourselves; we preach Christ Jesus, the Lord. All we say about ourselves is that we are your servants because of what Jesus has done for us. ⁶For God, who said, "Let there be light in the darkness," has made us understand that this light is the brightness of the glory of God that is seen in the face of Jesus Christ.

⁷But this precious treasure—this light and power that now shine within us—is held in perishable containers, that is, in our weak bodies.* So everyone can see that our glorious power is from God and is not our own.

⁸We are pressed on every side by troubles, but we are not crushed and broken. We are perplexed, but we don't

4:7 Greek *But we have this treasure in earthen vessels.*

give up and quit. ⁹We are hunted down, but God never abandons us. We get knocked down, but we get up again and keep going. ¹⁰Through suffering, these bodies of ours constantly share in the death of Jesus so that the life of Jesus may also be seen in our bodies.

¹¹Yes, we live under constant danger of death because we serve Jesus, so that the life of Jesus will be obvious in our dying bodies. ¹²So we live in the face of death, but it has resulted in eternal life for you.

Thought for the Day

The supremely valuable message of salvation in Jesus Christ has been entrusted by God to frail and fallible human beings. Paul's focus, however, was not on the perishable container but on its priceless contents—God's power dwelling in us. Though we are weak, God uses us to spread his Good News, and he gives us power to do his work. Knowing that the power is his, not ours, should keep us from pride and motivate us to keep daily contact with God, our power source. Our responsibility is to let people see God through us.

DAY 23

A Call to Imitate Jesus
Ephesians 4:17-32

¹⁷With the Lord's authority let me say this: Live no longer as the ungodly* do, for they are hopelessly

4:17 Greek *Gentiles.*

confused. [18]Their closed minds are full of darkness; they are far away from the life of God because they have shut their minds and hardened their hearts against him. [19]They don't care anymore about right and wrong, and they have given themselves over to immoral ways. Their lives are filled with all kinds of impurity and greed.

[20]But that isn't what you were taught when you learned about Christ. [21]Since you have heard all about him and have learned the truth that is in Jesus, [22]throw off your old evil nature and your former way of life, which is rotten through and through, full of lust and deception. [23]Instead, there must be a spiritual renewal of your thoughts and attitudes. [24]You must display a new nature because you are a new person, created in God's likeness—righteous, holy, and true.

[25]So put away all falsehood and "tell your neighbor the truth"* because we belong to each other. [26]And "don't sin by letting anger gain control over you."* Don't let the sun go down while you are still angry, [27]for anger gives a mighty foothold to the Devil.

[28]If you are a thief, stop stealing. Begin using your hands for honest work, and then give generously to others in need. [29]Don't use foul or abusive language. Let everything you say be good and helpful, so that your words will be an encouragement to those who hear them.

[30]And do not bring sorrow to God's Holy Spirit by the

4:25 Zech 8:16. 4:26 Ps 4:4.

way you live. Remember, he is the one who has identified you as his own, guaranteeing that you will be saved on the day of redemption.

³¹Get rid of all bitterness, rage, anger, harsh words, and slander, as well as all types of malicious behavior. ³²Instead, be kind to each other, tenderhearted, forgiving one another, just as God through Christ has forgiven you.

Thought for the Day

We can bring sorrow to the Holy Spirit by the way we live. Paul warns us against unwholesome language, bitterness, improper use of anger, harsh words, slander, and bad attitudes toward others. Instead of acting that way, we should be forgiving, just as God has forgiven us. Are you bringing sorrow or pleasing God with your attitudes and actions? Act in love toward your brothers and sisters in Christ, just as God acted in love by sending his Son to die for your sins.

DAY 24

Preparing for Spiritual Battle
Ephesians 6:10-20

¹⁰A final word: Be strong with the Lord's mighty power. ¹¹Put on all of God's armor so that you will be able to stand firm against all strategies and tricks of the Devil. ¹²For we are not fighting against people made of flesh and blood, but against the evil rulers and authorities

45

of the unseen world, against those mighty powers of darkness who rule this world, and against wicked spirits in the heavenly realms.

[13]Use every piece of God's armor to resist the enemy in the time of evil, so that after the battle you will still be standing firm. [14]Stand your ground, putting on the sturdy belt of truth and the body armor of God's righteousness. [15]For shoes, put on the peace that comes from the Good News, so that you will be fully prepared.* [16]In every battle you will need faith as your shield to stop the fiery arrows aimed at you by Satan.* [17]Put on salvation as your helmet, and take the sword of the Spirit, which is the Word of God. [18]Pray at all times and on every occasion in the power of the Holy Spirit. Stay alert and be persistent in your prayers for all Christians everywhere.

[19]And pray for me, too. Ask God to give me the right words as I boldly explain God's secret plan that the Good News is for the Gentiles, too.* [20]I am in chains now for preaching this message as God's ambassador. But pray that I will keep on speaking boldly for him, as I should.

Thought for the Day

Soldiers are trained to keep their equipment in battle-ready condition. Weapons are cleaned and oiled, communications equipment is checked and double-checked, and helmets are kept in place in case of sudden attack. If we

6:15 Or *For shoes, put on the readiness to preach the Good News of peace with God.* 6:16 Greek *by the evil one.* 6:19 Greek *explain the mystery of the gospel.*

prepare so diligently to face a human enemy, Paul says, how much more ought we to prepare for battle against our spiritual enemy? Satan will attack, he says, and only the believer who is grounded in the truth will recognize his lies. Only a personal acceptance by faith of God's love can protect our hearts from Satan's fiery temptations. Only a sure knowledge of salvation protects our minds from doubt. And only the Word of God and the power of Jesus Christ can cause Satan to flee in terror. Are you fully prepared for the battle?

DAY 25

A Call to Servanthood
Philippians 2:1-11

Is there any encouragement from belonging to Christ? Any comfort from his love? Any fellowship together in the Spirit? Are your hearts tender and sympathetic? ²Then make me truly happy by agreeing wholeheartedly with each other, loving one another, and working together with one heart and purpose.

³Don't be selfish; don't live to make a good impression on others. Be humble, thinking of others as better than yourself. ⁴Don't think only about your own affairs, but be interested in others, too, and what they are doing.

Christ's Humility and Exaltation
⁵Your attitude should be the same that Christ Jesus had. ⁶Though he was God, he did not demand and

cling to his rights as God. [7]He made himself nothing;* he took the humble position of a slave and appeared in human form.* [8]And in human form he obediently humbled himself even further by dying a criminal's death on a cross. [9]Because of this, God raised him up to the heights of heaven and gave him a name that is above every other name, [10]so that at the name of Jesus every knee will bow, in heaven and on earth and under the earth, [11]and every tongue will confess that Jesus Christ is Lord, to the glory of God the Father.

Thought for the Day

Jesus Christ was humble, willing to give up his rights in order to obey God and serve people. Like Christ, we should have a servant's attitude, serving out of love for God and for others, not out of guilt or fear. Remember, you can choose your attitude. You can approach life expecting to be served, or you can look for opportunities to serve others.

DAY 26

The Hope of the Resurrection
1 Thessalonians 4:13–5:11

[13]And now, brothers and sisters, I want you to know what will happen to the Christians who have died so you will not be full of sorrow like people who have no

2:7a Or *He laid aside his mighty power and glory.* 2:7b Greek *and was born in the likeness of men and was found in appearance as a man.*

hope. ¹⁴For since we believe that Jesus died and was raised to life again, we also believe that when Jesus comes, God will bring back with Jesus all the Christians who have died.

¹⁵I can tell you this directly from the Lord: We who are still living when the Lord returns will not rise to meet him ahead of those who are in their graves. ¹⁶For the Lord himself will come down from heaven with a commanding shout, with the call of the archangel, and with the trumpet call of God. First, all the Christians who have died will rise from their graves. ¹⁷Then, together with them, we who are still alive and remain on the earth will be caught up in the clouds to meet the Lord in the air and remain with him forever. ¹⁸So comfort and encourage each other with these words.

5 I really don't need to write to you about how and when all this will happen, ²for you know quite well that the day of the Lord will come unexpectedly, like a thief in the night. ³When people are saying, "All is well; everything is peaceful and secure," then disaster will fall upon them as suddenly as a woman's birth pains begin when her child is about to be born. And there will be no escape.

⁴But you aren't in the dark about these things, dear brothers and sisters, and you won't be surprised when the day of the Lord comes like a thief. ⁵For you are all children of the light and of the day; we don't

belong to darkness and night. ⁶So be on your guard, not asleep like the others. Stay alert and be sober. ⁷Night is the time for sleep and the time when people get drunk. ⁸But let us who live in the light think clearly, protected by the body armor of faith and love, and wearing as our helmet the confidence of our salvation. ⁹For God decided to save us through our Lord Jesus Christ, not to pour out his anger on us. ¹⁰He died for us so that we can live with him forever, whether we are dead or alive at the time of his return. ¹¹So encourage each other and build each other up, just as you are already doing.

Thought for the Day

Scholars have debated for centuries, and no doubt will continue to debate, over the events that will lead to Christ's return. What they don't debate nearly so much is that Jesus will come and what that coming means. It means for the believer that death is not a vast ending of nothingness and grief. It means for those who have placed their faith in Jesus Christ that there will be a great and glad reunion of joy and laughter—however and whenever Jesus returns. Therefore, although we are sorrowful and do grieve in the face of death, we have an unmistakable and unshakable hope as our sure foundation.

DAY 27

Fighting the Good Fight
2 Timothy 3:10–4:8

[10]But you know what I teach, Timothy, and how I live, and what my purpose in life is. You know my faith and how long I have suffered. You know my love and my patient endurance. [11]You know how much persecution and suffering I have endured. You know all about how I was persecuted in Antioch, Iconium, and Lystra—but the Lord delivered me from all of it. [12]Yes, and everyone who wants to live a godly life in Christ Jesus will suffer persecution. [13]But evil people and imposters will flourish. They will go on deceiving others, and they themselves will be deceived.

[14]But you must remain faithful to the things you have been taught. You know they are true, for you know you can trust those who taught you. [15]You have been taught the holy Scriptures from childhood, and they have given you the wisdom to receive the salvation that comes by trusting in Christ Jesus. [16]All Scripture is inspired by God and is useful to teach us what is true and to make us realize what is wrong in our lives. It straightens us out and teaches us to do what is right. [17]It is God's way of preparing us in every way, fully equipped for every good thing God wants us to do.

4 And so I solemnly urge you before God and before Christ Jesus—who will someday judge the living and

the dead when he appears to set up his Kingdom:
²Preach the word of God. Be persistent, whether the
time is favorable or not. Patiently correct, rebuke, and
encourage your people with good teaching.

³For a time is coming when people will no longer
listen to right teaching. They will follow their own
desires and will look for teachers who will tell them
whatever they want to hear. ⁴They will reject the truth
and follow strange myths.

⁵But you should keep a clear mind in every situation.
Don't be afraid of suffering for the Lord. Work at bringing others to Christ. Complete the ministry God has
given you.

Paul's Final Words
⁶As for me, my life has already been poured out as an
offering to God. The time of my death is near. ⁷I have
fought a good fight, I have finished the race, and I have
remained faithful. ⁸And now the prize awaits me—the
crown of righteousness that the Lord, the righteous
Judge, will give me on that great day of his return. And
the prize is not just for me but for all who eagerly look
forward to his glorious return.

Thought for the Day
  *Besieged by false teachers and the inevitable pres-
sures of a growing ministry, Timothy could easily have
abandoned his faith or modified his doctrine. Once
again Paul counseled Timothy to look to his past and
to hold to the basic teachings about Jesus that are*

eternally true. Like Timothy, we are surrounded by false teachings. But we must not allow our society to distort or crowd out God's eternal truth. Spend time every day reflecting on the foundation of your Christian faith found in God's Word, the great truths that build up your life.

DAY 28

Growing through Trying Times
James 1:2-18

²Dear brothers and sisters, whenever trouble comes your way, let it be an opportunity for joy. ³For when your faith is tested, your endurance has a chance to grow. ⁴So let it grow, for when your endurance is fully developed, you will be strong in character and ready for anything.

⁵If you need wisdom—if you want to know what God wants you to do—ask him, and he will gladly tell you. He will not resent your asking. ⁶But when you ask him, be sure that you really expect him to answer, for a doubtful mind is as unsettled as a wave of the sea that is driven and tossed by the wind. ⁷People like that should not expect to receive anything from the Lord. ⁸They can't make up their minds. They waver back and forth in everything they do.

⁹Christians who are* poor should be glad, for God has honored them. ¹⁰And those who are rich should be

1:9 Greek *The brother who is.*

glad, for God has humbled them. They will fade away like a flower in the field. ¹¹The hot sun rises and dries up the grass; the flower withers, and its beauty fades away. So also, wealthy people will fade away with all of their achievements.

¹²God blesses the people who patiently endure testing. Afterward they will receive the crown of life that God has promised to those who love him. ¹³And remember, no one who wants to do wrong should ever say, "God is tempting me." God is never tempted to do wrong, and he never tempts anyone else either. ¹⁴Temptation comes from the lure of our own evil desires. ¹⁵These evil desires lead to evil actions, and evil actions lead to death. ¹⁶So don't be misled, my dear brothers and sisters.

¹⁷Whatever is good and perfect comes to us from God above, who created all heaven's lights.* Unlike them, he never changes or casts shifting shadows. ¹⁸In his goodness he chose to make us his own children by giving us his true word. And we, out of all creation, became his choice possession.

Thought for the Day

One of the keys to growing and being able to effectively continue in the Christian life is endurance. A key aspect of endurance is patience. The word used for "endurance" in verse 3 is the Greek word hupomone, *which means "a patient enduring."*

1:17 Greek *from above, from the Father of lights.*

This cheerful, enduring patience, which helps us to continue in our Christian walk, actually comes—and develops—in times of testing and hardship. During these trials or "storms of life," our spiritual roots grow deeper, thus strengthening our faith. If we had our way, most of us would probably try to avoid these difficult times in our lives. Yet God promises that he will never give us more than we can handle (1 Corinthians 10:13).

These times of trial and testing will make us either better or bitter. It really is up to us and the outlook we choose to take. If we can learn to walk in our relationship with God on the basis of faith as opposed to mere feeling, we "will be strong in character and ready for anything."

DAY 29

Never Forget!
2 Peter 1:12-21

¹²I plan to keep on reminding you of these things—even though you already know them and are standing firm in the truth. ¹³Yes, I believe I should keep on reminding you of these things as long as I live. ¹⁴But the Lord Jesus Christ has shown me that my days here on earth are numbered and I am soon to die.* ¹⁵So I will work hard to make these things clear to you. I want you to remember them long after I am gone.

¹⁶For we were not making up clever stories when we

1:14 Greek *I must soon put off this earthly tent.*

told you about the power of our Lord Jesus Christ and his coming again. We have seen his majestic splendor with our own eyes. ¹⁷And he received honor and glory from God the Father when God's glorious, majestic voice called down from heaven, "This is my beloved Son; I am fully pleased with him." ¹⁸We ourselves heard the voice when we were there with him on the holy mountain.

¹⁹Because of that, we have even greater confidence in the message proclaimed by the prophets. Pay close attention to what they wrote, for their words are like a light shining in a dark place—until the day Christ appears and his brilliant light shines in your hearts.* ²⁰Above all, you must understand that no prophecy in Scripture ever came from the prophets themselves* ²¹or because they wanted to prophesy. It was the Holy Spirit who moved the prophets to speak from God.

Thought for the Day

Outstanding coaches constantly review the basics of the sport with their teams, and good athletes can execute the fundamentals consistently well. We must not neglect the basics of our faith when we go on to study deeper truths. Just as an athlete needs constant practice, we need constant reminders of the fundamentals of our faith and of how we came to believe in the first place. Don't allow yourself to be bored or impatient with messages on the basics of the Christian life. Instead, take the attitude

1:19 Or until the day dawns and the morning star rises in your hearts. 1:20 Or is a matter of one's own interpretation.

of an athlete who continues to practice and refine the basics even as he or she learns more advanced skills.

DAY 30

Loving One Another
1 John 4:7-21

⁷Dear friends, let us continue to love one another, for love comes from God. Anyone who loves is born of God and knows God. ⁸But anyone who does not love does not know God—for God is love.

⁹God showed how much he loved us by sending his only Son into the world so that we might have eternal life through him. ¹⁰This is real love. It is not that we loved God, but that he loved us and sent his Son as a sacrifice to take away our sins.

¹¹Dear friends, since God loved us that much, we surely ought to love each other. ¹²No one has ever seen God. But if we love each other, God lives in us, and his love has been brought to full expression through us.

¹³And God has given us his Spirit as proof that we live in him and he in us. ¹⁴Furthermore, we have seen with our own eyes and now testify that the Father sent his Son to be the Savior of the world. ¹⁵All who proclaim that Jesus is the Son of God have God living in them, and they live in God. ¹⁶We know how much God loves us, and we have put our trust in him.

God is love, and all who live in love live in God, and God lives in them. ¹⁷And as we live in God, our love grows more perfect. So we will not be afraid on the day of judgment, but we can face him with confidence because we are like Christ here in this world.

¹⁸Such love has no fear because perfect love expels all fear. If we are afraid, it is for fear of judgment, and this shows that his love has not been perfected in us. ¹⁹We love each other* as a result of his loving us first.

²⁰If someone says, "I love God," but hates another Christian,* that person is a liar; for if we don't love people we can see, how can we love God, whom we have not seen? ²¹And God himself has commanded that we must love not only him but our Christian brothers and sisters, too.

Thought for the Day

John says, "God is love," not "Love is God." Our world, with its shallow and selfish view of love, has turned these words around and contaminated our understanding of love. The world thinks that love is what makes a person feel good and that it is all right to sacrifice moral principles and others' rights in order to obtain such "love." But that isn't real love; it is the exact opposite—selfishness. And God is not that kind of "love." Real love is like God, who is holy, just, and perfect. If we truly know God, we will love as he does.

4:19 Or *We love him;* Greek reads *We love.* 4:20 Greek *brother.*

If you have enjoyed the Bible passages presented in *Living Words,* you can read the entire Bible text of the New Living Translation through a number of quality editions that help minister to a variety of spiritual needs.

New Living Translation Bible Editions

DELUXE TEXT EDITION

This special, clear-type text edition appeals to anyone who wants to experience God's Word through the New Living Translation. Providing readability with a warm and emotive style, the New Living Translation will touch you as if you were reading the Bible for the very first time. Available in stores in August 1996.

LIFE APPLICATION® STUDY BIBLE

This best-selling study Bible contains over 10,000 application notes to help you apply the truth of God's Word to everyday life. In addition, the *Life Application Study Bible* includes extensive book introductions, in-text maps and charts, personality profiles, a topical index, a concordance/dictionary, and words of Christ in red letter. Available in stores in October 1996.

TOUCHPOINT™ BIBLE

Never before has God's Word been so accessible to those who need it. The *TouchPoint Bible* quickly directs you to specific passages in God's Word to help meet an immediate need in your life. At the center of the *TouchPoint Bible* is the Helpfinder, a comprehensive reference system that contains hundreds of the most heartfelt issues people face today. Available in stores in October 1996.

NEW BELIEVER'S™ BIBLE

Whether you are a new Christian looking for answers or a seasoned believer who wants to review the biblical foundations, the *New Believer's Bible* presents the basics of Christianity in a way that is easy to follow. Four study tracks written by pastor and evangelist Greg Laurie are incorporated within the Bible text and take you through specific portions of Scripture. Available in stores in November 1996. The *New Believer's Bible* is also available in a New Testament edition, which will be available in August 1996.

THE ONE YEAR® BIBLE

Through a unique and easy-to-use format, *The One Year Bible* gives you an organized method of reading through the entire Bible in one year! Each 15-minute daily reading combines portions of the Old Testament, New Testament, Psalms, and Proverbs to give you a unique balance of Scripture. Available in stores in November 1996.

BIBLE ON CASSETTE

The beauty of the language and style of the New Living Translation comes alive through this dramatic, multivoiced presentation. Featuring sound effects, original music, and professional actors, this digitally mastered recording is perfect to play at home, in the office, or on the road. The *Bible on Cassette* is available in a complete Bible edition and a New Testament edition. Available in stores in October 1996.